"Running True"

A Model for Organizational Alignment

Curt M. Thompson, Ph.D.

ISBN: 0615781551
ISBN-13: **978-0615781556**

DEDICATION

TO MY PARENTS - THEIR EXAMPLE OF ALWAYS "RUNNING TRUE" WILL SHAPE THE LIVES OF THEIR CHILDREN AND GRANDCHILDREN FOREVER.

TO MY WIFE HEIDI WHO ALWAYS RISES TO MEET THE STANDARD OF RUNNING TRUE IN ALL THAT SHE DOES.

CONTENTS

ACKNOWLEDGMENTS

I would like to express my sincere thanks to the many people who inspired me to write this book. Through their teaching, support, discussions, comments and assistance in editing and proofreading, my ideas are now a reality.

In particular I would like to thank my wife and children for their unconditional support and my siblings for giving me the kick in the rear that I needed to complete the project.

Curt M. Thompson, Ph.D.

INTRODUCTION

If a company or organization is smart the people who run it will realize the time to get things right is when starting out. By right, I mean a company that has built into the culture an environment of learning and change. One that values people and realizes they make up the organization.

One that has a systematic way to improve and evolve based upon response to suggestions of improvement as well as responding to current market conditions. Those organizations that have done these things will be more prepared to be profitable in a downturn in the market. Why? Because these organizations have a renewal mechanism built in wherein they strive for perfection in all economic environments.

These organizations are lean, aligned, and streamlined. These organizations transform themselves in the times of plenty by simplifying, streamlining, rightsizing, and so on, to survive and thrive in the market lean times. These organizations will be the organizations of tomorrow because they are smart organizations today. Only the smart organizations will live to meet another day.

Chapter One - Leadership Alignment

When conducting management training on Leadership Alignment I ask if anyone owns or has owned a business. I then ask if they employ or have employed any other people in that business. Most always, there are those who have.

When asked what they expect of their employees. The following are typical of the responses I have received:

- Honesty is usually at the top of the list.
- Integrity
- Hard work
- Knowledge
- Friendly to the customers

- Problem solvers
- Truthful
- Willing to seek guidance
- Team players
- Get along well with others
- Thrifty
- Deliver on time

I then ask what the word alignment means:

To begin the discussion, I ask, "What is done to a car when a mechanic aligns the wheels?" The best answer I have received is, "They adjust the front and rear wheels so they run true with each other." To run true! It is the desire of any business owner or leader to want their people to run true with the company's mission, goals, values and principles?

It is my goal as an author, trainer and consultant to provide tools to enable the people within organizations to create an organizational culture where actions "run true" or are aligned to the vision and guiding principles.

After discussing the meaning of alignment I display

on a PowerPoint slide the guiding principles and values of the leadership & owners of the company for which they work. I then have someone read these written guiding principles and values, asking those in attendance to pay attention to their gut reaction, thoughts and feelings as it is read. Most participants agree that the list of desirable employee traits listed were actually compatible with their own personal guiding principles and values. To boil it all down, leadership wants people who will "Run True" even when they are not there to steer or guide them!

Alignment Rating Scale

After reviewing the organizations current guiding principles and values I display an alignment rating scale used to determine the perception of members of the organization regarding organizational alignment. The participants are asked where they would rate themselves or their department.

There are two potentials on the rating scale:

1. That is totally true it is our world:

This means that what is written by upper management or business owners is actually being lived and delivered on their level or division of the organization.

2. Not true at all it is their world:

This means that what goes on at this level or division of the organization is not what is written or talked about in the upper part of the organization. They may believe it there but it is not delivered here!

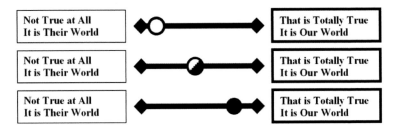

The dot to the far left is an empty dot indicating a bad place to stop. The middle dot is a half-filled dot indicating warning/caution and again is not where we want to be. The dot to the far right is filled indicating that this is where we want to be/go.

Empty dot:

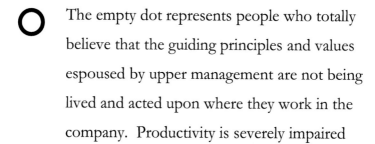 The empty dot represents people who totally believe that the guiding principles and values espoused by upper management are not being lived and acted upon where they work in the company. Productivity is severely impaired with respect to what could be accomplished.

Half-filled dot:

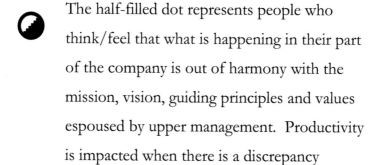 The half-filled dot represents people who think/feel that what is happening in their part of the company is out of harmony with the mission, vision, guiding principles and values espoused by upper management. Productivity is impacted when there is a discrepancy between what is written and what is done.

Filled dot:

The filled dot represents people who think/feel that what is happening in their department is in alignment with the principles and values of the upper leadership.

Productivity and job satisfaction are at the highest levels when alignment is achieved.

The results of this brief exercise can be used as a starting point for planning and discussion. It is particularly useful to identify and seriously reflect on the concerns of those who feel at odds with the actions and events occurring within the department in which they work. The goal of "Running True" requires leadership to design an organization where everyone is functioning in the realm of: "It is totally true, it is our world."

It takes a courageous leader to even ask because what is often discovered is that the team runs to where they think they are being lead.

The Five-Box Model of Leadership Alignment
Leadership Integrity Model

A five-box model can illustrate leadership alignment. Four of the five boxes represent cornerstones and the fifth represents the capstone. Perhaps little attention is paid to the cornerstones of leadership alignment while much attention is given to the outcome or what is done. That is placing the cart in front of the horse.

Front View

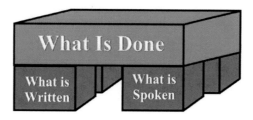

Rear View

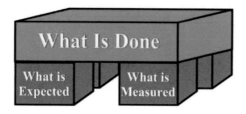

If the leadership has methodically placed the four cornerstones of leadership by posting, talking about, expecting, measuring and rewarding; the capstone is almost automatically placed or assured that what is written, talked about, expected, measured and rewarded is what is actually being done.

Leadership alignment exists when all boxes are in

balance. It becomes a synergistic equation where the sum or outcome/benefit is greater than the parts. For this to occur, each outcome must be equal or aligned with the previous part or input. Each one of these boxes also represents methods by which Smart Leaders steer the organization. The meaning of the concept of steering mechanisms will be discussed in each of the following chapters. One of the paramount goals of organizations is to be productive. If any of these elements are not in alignment, productivity decreases or will be impaired.

Leadership Alignment Model

Leadership alignment can also be displayed by utilizing the following method and model:

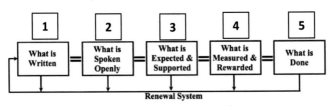

Smart Organizations By Design Alignment Model, © 2002

Box One What is written:

1 • Organizations, schools, government often have mission statements, guiding principles, policies, procedures, best practices, etc., all of which are written down.

• These are placed on walls, in policy manuals, reports to shareholders, etc.

Box Two What is Spoken:

2 • Most everyone talks about the written and published items openly in organizational meetings.

Box Three What is Expected and Supported:

3 • For a Leader to be in alignment they must expect themselves and those they lead to carry out written organizational mission statements, guiding principles, policies, procedures, best practices, etc., day in and day out.

• A leader must supply the necessary support in guidance, supplies, materials,

etc., needed to carry out what is
expected.

Box Four What is Measured and Rewarded:

4 • The Leader measures and rewards efforts
that are in alignment with organizational
mission statements, guiding principles,
policies, procedures, best practices, etc.,
day in and day out.

Box Five What is Done:

5 • What is done is delivered through the
actions of writing, talking about, expecting,
measuring and rewarding.

Renewal System:

- The quest of the renewal system is to
make sure that what is written in the
mission, guiding principles, strategic
business plan, etc., are being reflected in
the end result of what is actually done and
delivered.

- If there is a notable gap between what is
envisioned and the result, an analysis of
each of the five boxes must be undertaken

to determine where and what the disconnects are.

- The renewal process analyzes each area to ascertain if there are any disconnects or gaps and take any corrective action as needed.

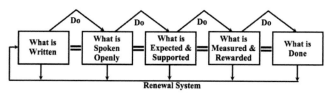

Smart Organizations By Design Alignment Model Expanded, © 2002

Do/Action:

For any organizational system to be successful, it requires aligned doing or action from start to completion. The "do" arrows were added for clarification and additional insight of the meaning of the = signs in the model. Do=Action step. For example, if the action step that naturally follows "what is written" is not taken performance will suffer and will eventually be out of alignment. If "what is spoken openly" is not converted to expectation and supported, performance and alignment will suffer. If "what is done" does not flow from "what is measured and rewarded"; performance will be in

11

failure mode. If "what is done" is not followed by assessment or the renewal system to improve and steer performance; opportunity to improve or evolve based upon current conditions will be lost.

What is written?

CHAPTER TWO - WHAT IS WRITTEN

Are the guiding principles and values of your organization written?

Organizations are initiated or started from a single individual's vision, values and guiding principles. The person may have close associations with other people who also buy into the vision or help shape it. If these people remain in alignment and have a good organizational structure, strategy, product or service, the organization grows and prospers. As the organization grows by becoming larger, often the values and principles of the founding leaders are replaced with a focus on shareholder value and more and more policies and procedures; the work becomes just work without vision, purpose or feeling. The

organization transforms into one with many words
and little guidance.

If, as business leaders or owners, you are making it
clear to the lower rank and file that your main effort
is to increase shareholder value you will anger them!
There will be an increased potential of a subculture
of passive aggressive behavior and resistance. Why?
Because each person is giving a good portion of his
or her life to work, to deliver this message is
arrogant, uncaring, rude and simply uninspiring!
Every person who works is trying to build something
for themselves and the families they are trying to
raise. People want to be cared about and to
contribute to something worthwhile through the
work they perform.

With a truthful vision and purpose that portrays each
person as being worthwhile, deserving and needed;
one of the natural outcomes will be maximized
shareholder value and not the other way around!

Rank and file members can appreciate the fact that
the opportunity for employment has come to them

because people have invested their money into the organization. To start any organization, capital must be expended and those who have expended that capital are expecting to have a return on their investment, indeed they deserve a return.

One of the ultimate costs for everything is time and life! People on the front line are giving their time and ultimately their life to work and some are giving more and at higher costs. A research article alleged that construction workers have a lower life expectancy than the general population. This may be more or less so in other occupations. There is also research evidence that shows certain stress can affect life expectancies and illness, management as well as others certainly may be affected. The vision, mission and guiding principles must be distilled down to concrete and actionable steps to engage every member in both heart and mind. This is where organizations move forward in an enduring and sustainable manner.

CHAPTER THREE –
WHAT IS SPOKEN OR TALKED ABOUT?

Are the guiding principles and values of your organization spoken and talked about?

Talking about it:

Someone once said talking is easy…well maybe not, it can be hard.

Do you actually talk about the written mission statements, guiding principles, policies, procedures, and best practices or are they just left on the wall or in books? In your meetings do you bring them up and talk about them? Are they on your agendas? Do you ask if what has been done or being done on a day-to-day basis is in alignment with them? If not you are not steering you organizations as it could be! The verbalization of important company values provides an opportunity to be used as a steering mechanism.

It is important for all levels of management to post the guiding principles, talk about them and act upon them daily. Only in this way will everyone throughout the organization take them seriously. One of the major ways in which leaders steer the organization and influence it is to actually to do what they say.

Leadership Alignment Strategy:

In order for the mission, guiding principles and values of the leadership to be known internally and externally to the organization they must be published and talked about. Delivery mechanisms must be utilized to get the word out. We are not talking about what spin-doctors and media experts tell you in order to create an awareness of the company based upon what management and consumers may want to hear as derived from public opinion polls. We are talking serious down to earth simple truths of what principles are truly espoused and placed into action day by day! Now, there is nothing wrong with using PR Departments or contracted media professionals to get the word out regarding the positive attributes of your organization if the information portrayed is true and accurate.

Dissemination of Information:

Speech within an organization must be in alignment with the vision, mission, guiding principles, and values and must be deliverable and actionable. The goal of speech or what is spoken must be to translate these into actionable steps.

When what is spoken is not in harmony with the vision, mission, guiding principles, and values it creates an environment of mistrust among members, especially frontline employees.

Organizational engagement from your members will begin to become seriously impaired if what is spoken is not aligned with what is written but it can't just be sent out or passed along, it must be delivered! People do not like to work for a leader that just passes things on. They will follow and lead with safety and integrity when they have a leader that can speak and act with integrity. People want to be engaged in their work and believe they have an important role to play in the organization. Help make it easy for them by providing them with an honest straightforward approach where what is spoken is aligned with what is written!

Not just for the office:

For the sake of clarity we are assuming that the guiding principles of the leadership are genuine and not false or a façade, meaning that they expect all levels of the organization to live by them. Living is doing...

I know of a mine supervisor who went into an underground miner's workplace and noticed some rock about to fall. He yelled for miner to move! Just after he moved a large boulder fell. The miner said, "That was the best safety talk you ever gave me!"

For example:

In one meeting when asked, "Are we delivering on our mission and guiding principles day in and day out?" One person said, "I don't think we are consistent in the area of fostering teamwork. Our reward system still delivers greater rewards to

individual people and team members have noticed."
That is saying one thing and doing another!

Corrective steering required:

The following problems were discovered:

- Not all team members were pulling their weight.

- Individuals were being rewarded which was one reason why people wanted to do their own thing.

- People withheld information when it could have helped another team member because they wanted the reward the information could bring or if the information was withheld the other person who needed the information would not get an opportunity to shine above the member who withheld it.

The following solutions delivered.

- The individual rewards were minimized and the team rewards were maximized.

- The team would agree upon what was to be expected from each team member and if not delivered the member would be asked about it and helped to improve. If the member did not improve they were asked to leave the team. Arbitrators could/would be used to ensure both sides were fairly represented in difficult cases.

- Information was shared with everyone.

As one gets older and unmistakably realizes how fragile mortality is they seem to want to leave a legacy of honor where their word and work has meant something and that they were or are a part of something that made or makes a difference to people and their lives. Again, organizations do not exist, people do. Organizations only exist as long as there are people filling roles within that organization.

CHAPTER FOUR - WHAT IS EXPECTED AND SUPPORTED?

Are the guiding principles and values of your organization written, spoken, talked about, supported and then expected to be carried out?

To promote and foster leadership alignment leaders must have the expectation that all members of the organization will act in harmony with what is written and spoken. The examination and awareness of how this aligns in your organization is an exceptional tool if it is used as a steering mechanism.

If expectations from leaders are based on what is written and spoken, most people will steer their actions and behaviors to deliver on them. You have to be very clear with your expectations and they must be in harmony with what is written, and spoken openly. Of course you can steer your division or department as you wish but if it is not in line with the guiding principles of the organization as a whole, you will eventually be in trouble.

The following is an interesting example of one manager who clearly expected something different than what was written or spoken openly:

> On one occasion I was told to do something that was against written or spoken company policy, so I asked the manager, "How can I carry that out?" He asked, "What do you mean?" I said, "Based upon the actual work situation if I did what you asked then I will be out of compliance with company policy and procedure." He got a bit irritable and said, "Well it has to be done." I asked, "Do you want me to do it?" He said in a flustered manner, "Well I just don't want to see you do it," and jumped in his vehicle and drove off.

This manager sent a message loud and clear that he had another agenda, one that was not according to what was written in company policy! He also proved that he could not be trusted and would leave me to hang if I did what he actually wanted and got caught by someone who would enforce the rules or policy. This sort of thing falls into what can be referred to as an evaporative event. This supervisor's words, just as mine, had disappeared into sound waves leaving no record of the interaction between us, therefore I could not provide any proof if I was questioned as to why I was violating company policy. The proof of words disappears as evaporating water leaving no proof of the water or of words spoken.

Realistic Expectations come after Support is provided:

One can expect something to be done but it is another thing to be able to realistically expect it to be carried out. Unless the required support is given, one cannot realistically expect what is desired. Yes, there can be lot of irrational expectations from managers and others expecting miracles to be performed. A person should only realistically expect something after they have provided the needed training, expertise, materials, time, and all other required items or methodologies needed to deliver it. You may irrationally expect it, but figs do not come from thistles!

If you ask a person to dig a ditch and do not provide a shovel what will happen?

In my estimation, teachers are one of the unappreciated professions in the area of pay. But the insults do not end there. I have heard told by more than one teacher and prospective teacher that they are required to teach subjects without books! This is amazing, asking teachers to do better, asking teachers to deliver students who can pass tests, asking teachers to be qualified but not giving them support! This is all too common and is bitterly sad! What do many of the teachers do? They purchase supplies out of their own sparsely filled pockets

I worked at a company where assignments were given

for the day's work but every day you would get to the work area only to find that the tools or supplies to do the job would not be there. Two hours each day or more would be wasted looking for the supplies or tools needed to complete the job. Both leadership and front line workers were frustrated.

Due to my frustration and my false belief that we were a team with the goal of increasing productivity, I developed a work area readiness checklist that people could fill out at the end of shift and hand it in to the shift boss. On the form people could document what work was in process, what supplies or equipment was needed, what if any safety concerns existed and so on. With this information, the shift boss could make the necessary arrangements to get the supplies and tools for the next crew coming on. By using this system everyone would know what is needed before they got to the work area thus increasing productivity, lessening frustration and potentially providing greater profit to the company and bonuses for the employees.

When I presented the one page form to middle

management the person said, "I think we are doing fine." In other words, do not bother me with that! I could not believe it. When I hired on, wonderful videos and propaganda were presented in their new employee orientation representing the company as a place that: had an open door policy, wanted participation from everyone, and that they cared about each member, and so on. What was written and spoken during training was far from what was being lived at the front line.

This company was making very large profits in spite of these problems, which made it an opportune time to really get it organized. Their belief was that they were doing great and did not want to be bothered; therefore the door to change was closed! The cycle of business always turns or changes. Gold prices are up and then they go down. Gold ore is easy to access but later it may be harder to access and more costly.

CHAPTER FIVE - WHAT IS MEASURED AND REWARDED?

Are the guiding principles and values of your organization spoken, talked about, expected to be carried out and then measured and rewarded?

On occasion I will hear managers say, "What reward?" They get paid to do the job - that is their reward! These people just don't get it. The paycheck is a reward that is given too late to matter in a substantial way! I have concluded that the largest percentages of the people who feel that the paycheck is the reward are very poor at giving out any kind of recognition.

Motivation vs. demotivation

Studies indicate that pay is not a motivator, it is a de-motivator. What does that mean? Well, evaluate what you think about day in and day out. What thoughts do you have? What generates feelings of satisfaction? Most people conclude it is what they do hour-by-hour that creates a feeling of job satisfaction. To create that overall satisfaction it is important to know what the game is and how it is scored. Knowing that if a certain amount of work done each day will meet or exceed the daily, weekly, monthly, quarterly, and yearly business outcome targets is motivational. However employees who think they have met organizational targets, by meeting or exceeding what they think is required of them, but do not get paid accordingly will be in a de-motivated state of mind.

In addition, if the pay is not in line with job duties and the going rate industry-wide, it will produce a higher probability for worker demotivation. In reality motivation comes from both intrinsic and extrinsic rewards.

One can expect what they inspect.

Most rewards that foster motivation and leadership alignment cost nothing in dollar amounts to deliver. Saying things like, "Joe you did a good job that was exactly like I wanted it! This work area is very much in order, the travel and walkways are clear, the work bench is organized, the lids are on the trash cans," and so on.

Targeted Feedback:

Leaders must know what the business targets are and know how they can foster a climate that will facilitate meeting them most of the time. For example managers who know how to do this can be heard saying things like the following vignettes: The following vignettes illustrate positive interactions geared toward providing meaningful feedback.

Safety:

"I see you have taken care of the ventilation problem that was on the list this morning. Thanks for taking care of that before starting on production!"

Environment:

"I noticed that you reported that fuel spill and then took the time to clean it up. I know it put you behind on your production goal but you did the responsible thing and took take care of the spill first. Thanks. By the way, what do you think we could do in order to make sure that it never happens again?"

Production:

"Jane, you are six loads over the shift halfway target, you are really on a roll and all the loads meet our customer requirements." Great job! "Jane replies, Even after shutting down in time to service the equipment and clean up my work area I still should exceed the target by ten loads." "That is excellent, it is important to give the other shift a good hand off (A clean work area and serviced equipment)!"

Waste Reduction:

"Jane, I noticed that you wound that piece of wire back onto the new spool where it can be used. A lot of people are throwing that short stuff away; it costs three dollars a foot." "Jane replies saying, "I know the short pieces of this wire are used at least two times per day." "Thanks again Jane great job!"

Motivational Steering:

What do these vignettes tell us? They tell us that these types of rewards and measures will create and support a climate where leadership is helping to steer the organization to meet and exceed projected targets. People like to work for organizations where the leadership knows what the targets/goals are and tells everyone what they are. They tell people when they are scoring and what the score is. They tell people when they are not scoring and coach them regarding what they can do to start scoring again. They do these things daily! People like to work where they know what the game is, how the game is being scored and what they personally can do to score and win every day! One can begin to see why thinking that the paycheck is a reward is far too late to be an effective steering mechanism for motivation and in meeting or exceeding organizational targets.

Many people do not like managers looking over their shoulder to see if they are doing what needs to be done. These people may be responding to the manager's methods rather than the fact that they are being observed. If the manager is using observation as a weapon it is threatening and de-motivational. If the observation is used as a tool to recognize and reward workers for doing a good job or to coach them in a way that helps them score, motivation is the result.

Performance appraisals:

Many people are surprised when performance appraisal time comes. They think they have been doing a good job and actually maybe right. The disconnect, comes when the performance goals have not been made clear and the manager has been looking at something else, another agenda or target. The manager has not taken time to do motivational steering nor explain what the organizational daily targets are and how they break down into daily individual targets. To make things worse, perhaps the manager really does not know himself or herself, which makes evaluation of employees very subjective rather than objective. Often people accuse a manager of showing favoritism to those they like the most and they may have a point, if subjective rather than objective targets and measures are being utilized.

Smart Performance Appraisals:

Smart performance appraisals are developed from making the organization's vision, guiding principles and values actionable at all levels of the organization. It is vitally necessary for front-line employees to know without equivocation that the actions they take day-to-day are in alignment with the company mission and are without doubt in alignment with the expectations of their direct supervisor.

With this alignment one can expect that each employee can be in a state of organizational engagement. Just as in adult learning methodology one of the basic tenets of learning is that adults need to know why they need to learn or know something. So it is with organizational engagement, adults need to know that the actions they take makes a difference and are in alignment with the vision, guiding principles and values of the organization from top to bottom.

One associate wrote this note about performance appraisals: "An excellent method of appraisal would be to allow the employee to conduct a self-appraisal. Most employees are self-critical and will provide more objective critique. After the employee self-appraises, then the employee and manager can sit down together to review the appraisal and set mutually agreed upon goals for future performance. It is also important to ensure that the appraisal covers the entire appraisal period in measuring performance. Some managers' focus on an event that occurred close to appraisal time and disregard the other eleven months of performance be it a good or bad event.

When in a state of alignment or engagement each person can give himself or herself an appraisal each day or week. The most powerful thing about self-appraisal is that this becomes a steering mechanism for every person engaged in the organization. They know if they are hitting the mark hour by hour and can make any needed corrective steering long before any not so smart organizations dole out the six-month or yearly performance appraisal or productivity is affected! I don't think that it takes anyone of exceptional insight to see and know the truth of this point! Yet the big question is why this is so rare?

```
┌─────────────────────┐
│                     │
│   What is Done?     │
│                     │
└─────────────────────┘
```

CHAPTER SIX - WHAT IS DONE?

Are the guiding principles and values of your organization spoken, talked about, and then expected to be carried out, measured, rewarded and finally actually done?

In the end, leadership in organizations will get the things done that they actually in reality expect, measure and reward. If you are an organizational owner or a leader in general and are not getting the things done that you expect, then this is for you. Use the leadership alignment model to trace out where the root of the problem lies. Think of each box as a potential steering mechanism, we say potential because it is just that, a potential until someone actually does so.

There are so many dollars wasted in corporations on training, consultants, and so on, not because it is not valuable information, but because it is not used and put into practice throughout the organization. There is perhaps nothing really overwhelmingly new here this is simple stuff. Just as it is, when I read books from other authors or when I hear what other consultants have to say in most cases I can trace what they are selling back many years prior to a more original theorist. I use more original because no one lives in a vacuum or has come up with anything totally without inspiration from other people or based upon their reaction to the environment in which they live. More power to them if they package it just right and get people to use it. A moderate plan that is used and fully implemented will yield much higher returns than an exceptional plan that is not utilized.

Example:

I have noticed that organizational settings seem to be getting more complex and sophisticated, perhaps beyond good sense. More and more programs or procedures are implemented and important items start being missed. When this happens I ask the question or make a statement - "What is the simplest thing that can be done to take us to the Promised Land?" People act like they need them all (old programs and new programs) but upon closer analysis when things were simpler they were not doing those things day by day either and now when they are more complex they can't possibly do it! Why do people bring in more and more new procedures? Because things were not getting done! Why? Because they did not act upon what they already had! They did not talk about it, they did not expect it, they did not measure it and reward it, and finally it was not done! Is there any real wonder and amazement as you read this? Now this is an over simplification, the utilization of more complete Organizational Design methods and tools have helped create exceptional results and will do so in the future. The point is that there are many different flavors of the month and many of them could have delivered results if they were accepted and implemented with enduring consistency.

```
┌─────────────────────────┐
│                         │
│     Renewal System      │
│                         │
└─────────────────────────┘
```

CHAPTER SEVEN - RENEWAL SYSTEM

Smart Leaders Steer for Results:

Leaders utilize all components of the five-box model
to steer the actions and outcomes of the
organization, which are the production and actions of
individual people. They understand the power and
leveraged outcomes that can be achieved by utilizing
each cornerstone and capstone of the alignment
model as steering mechanisms.

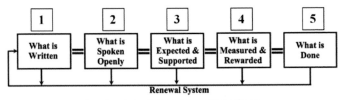

Smart Organizations By Design Alignment Model, © 2002

The quest of the renewal system is to make sure that what is written in the mission, guiding principles, strategic business plan, etc., are being reflected in the end result of what is actually being done and delivered. If there is a notable gap between what is envisioned and the results produced, an analysis of each of the five boxes must be undertaken to determine where and what the disconnects are.

Renewal System Basic Details:

The renewal system as shown in the model has an arrow coming out from each box. It is important to analyze each when there are significant gaps between what is written and what is actually done. A determination of the nature of disconnects and the corrective action(s) required is vital to the health of the organization.

ADVANCED ORGANIZATIONAL TOOLS

For help with the concepts contained in this book, please contact the Author. The usefulness of this model goes beyond organizational mission and values; it is a useful tool to assess the alignment and effectiveness of your policies and procedures including your systems and processes.

Specialties: Human Resources, Safety, Training, Organizational Development, Human and Organizational Performance Improvement, Advanced Knowledge & Practical Application of Human Psychological and Physical Capabilities that has achieved improved performance and reduction of human error, Performance Improvement methodologies which include Human Performance Improvement, Change Management, Organizational Systems Design, Lean Six Sigma, etc.

Inquiries are welcome:

curt@smartorganizations or curt@safetyculture.com

ABOUT THE AUTHOR

Curt M. Thompson is gifted in the area of Organizational Systems Design, including:

- Training & Development Leadership
- Quality & Performance Improvement
- Long-Range Business Planning
- HR Strategic Direction
- Organizational Surveys
- Performance Solution Implementation
- Organization Design & Development
- Interpersonal Communications Solutions
- Organizational Performance Assessment
- Training program set up/implementation
- Process Mapping and Silo Identification

He has worked with mining companies, government agencies, and restaurants; written hundreds of training manuals; developed human performance tool instructional materials and instructed and coached over 800 managers and frontline personnel in the use of the tools.

Curt has a **Ph.D. in Industrial and Organizational Behavior and Leadership** from United States International University, San Diego, California and has additional training in:

- Implementation Management Training and Accreditation *AIM* Implementation Management Methodology, Implementation Management Associates, Inc. 2009
- Lean Six Sigma Training 2007 Project ROI $200K. Black Belt 2008.
- Making the Transition to Performance Improvement, ISPI 2007.
- Senior Professional in Human Resources (SPHR), HRCI 2004.
- Certified Performance Technologist (CPT), ASTD and ISPI 2003.
- Training Certificate ASTD, 2002.
- Human and Organizational Performance Improvement (HPI) certificate, ASTD 2004.
    - Human Performance Improvement in the Workplace, ASTD.
    - Analyzing Human and Organizational Performance, ASTD.
    - Selecting and Managing Performance Improvement Interventions, ASTD.
    - Evaluating Performance Improvement Interventions, ASTD.
    - Transitioning to Human Performance Improvement, ASTD.
- TAPROOT trained for root cause analysis.
- Return on Investment (ROI) Certificate, Jack Phillips 2004.
- Corporate Systems Design, CSD, Inc. 2001.
- Certified in Situational Leadership, Center for Leadership Studies. 2002

- 7 Habits, Franklin Covey 2002.
- Certified in Crucial Conversation training and Influencer training, Vital Smarts.
- Social Styles (Analytical, Driver, Amiable and Expressive), TRACOM 2003.
- MSHA Approved Instructor IU and IS of 30 CFR, Part 48, Subpart A & B.

He is dedicated to assisting organizations large or small to develop into "Smart Organizations" with all systems aligned. For more information visit his website at www.smartorganizations.com.